# The Javascript Adventure

## Learn to Code by Building a Text-based Adventure Game

# The Javascript Adventure

### Learn to Code by Building a Text-based Adventure Game

**Ron Sims II**
**2015**

**The Javascript Adventure**
**Learn to Code by Building a Text-based Adventure Game**

Published by the author Ron Sims II 2015

First published by the author June 2015

For information related to educational and institutional sales please contact :
ron@orangemantis.net
216.365.8223

Source code for the examples in this book are available at:
https://github.com/orangemantis/gamekit/archive/master.zip

# Introduction

This book was created to help people get started writing computer code. Every attempt was made to keep things as simple as possible. To do this, many concepts are not covered because frankly they make things way too complicated. This is not a guide to teach all things programming. It is just a book that helps people get started.

The concepts in this book are taught by showing you how to build a game. Just about every line you write will contribute to creating a simple text-based adventure game. All you will need to get started is a computer with Google's Chrome browser, a text editor, an internet connection (to download the starter materials) and a bit of imagination.

Chapters 1-6 of this book are designed with the beginner in mind. These sections teach the reader how to write game code from scratch. The examples found in the first six chapters introduce the Javascript language and many key programming concepts.

Chapters 7-8 are for intermediate learners that have mastered the concepts introduced in the first part of the book. This part of the book breaks down how the included sample game works.

## A Note on Format

The section below explains the text format of this book.

---

**New technical terms, important concepts and things to remember are in bold.**

*Technical terms and important concepts are italicized.*

```
Code appears in this font.
```

```
New code that you must add is in this font and bold!
```

---

This is really all you need to know to get started. If you have a question, feel free to send me a tweet **@mantisorange**. Keep reading and within minutes you will have written your first program!

# Chapter 1: Hello World, Everybody's First Program

Computer programming is not hard, it just takes time. Don't worry, it will be fun (most of the time). Enough talk, let's get busy coding. All you need to start is a modern **web browser** and a basic **text editor**. Fortunately, most computers already have both of these installed.

---

**Note:** For Windows we recommend using the **Notepad++** text editor. For Mac we recommend the **Text Wrangler** editor. **Google's Chrome** is recommended for both platforms.

---

Let's write your first program.

1. Open your browser and navigate to google.com (type "http://google.com" in the address bar and press enter).

2. Right click on the page and select **Inspect element** from the context menu.

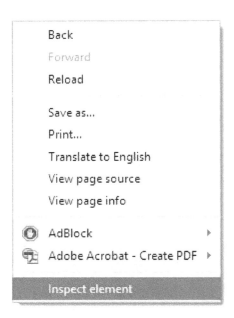

The browser window should now be split. One part of the screen should still show the Google page and the other should have a bunch of technical options like: *Network, Console, Elements* and so on. This is the **inspector**. The *inspector* is the main tool in the browser used for programming.

3. In the Inspector look for a tab labeled **Console** and click on it. The *console* is where you make the programming magic happen.

4. Typically somewhere in the console you will see **>**. This is called the **console prompt**, or *prompt* for short.

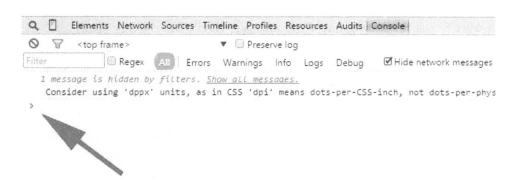

In computerese (the strange technical vocabulary of programming) the *console* is where you type **commands**, things you want the computers to do.

5. Type this at the *prompt and hit enter:*

**alert("Hello World");**

If you typed everything correctly, a window should have popped up that said "Hello World".

Congratulations! You have just written your first program. Let's talk about what you just did.

The *console* that lives inside the *inspector* is the place where any valid commands will be executed. Anything that you type there that follows the rules of Javascript will be evaluated and performed.

You basically told the browser to tell the user to show the message "Hello World". You did this by using the **alert function**. A **function**, sometimes called a **method,** is special code that tells the computer to do something specific. *Functions* are the verbs of computer languages. You may notice that there are parenthesis after the word alert. The parenthesis are a dead giveaway that you are using function. Whatever you put in the parenthesis can be used by the function. In computerese, the thing you put in the parenthesis is called a **parameter** or **param** for short.

In the case of the *alert* function, you can put any words in the parenthesis and the browser will popup a window showing whatever you typed. In computerese, words are called **strings**. A string must begin and end with quotes. The quotes tell the computer to just read the text.

In the *console* type:

**alert(Hello World);**

When you hit enter you should see a nasty error. The browser is confused because it expected "Hello World" and got Hello World (no quotes).

Lastly, you ended the command with a semicolon. In Javascript a semicolon is like period at the end of a sentence. It tells the browser that the command statement is done. Semicolons are used to separate **statements** like periods separate sentences.

We will explore functions and *strings* in detail later. For now get comfortable using alerts. Did you know that you can type several alerts in a row to create a series of messages?

```
alert("Who's afraid of the big bad wolf?");
alert("3 little piggies!");
```

**Note:** To type multiple line of code in the *console* without running them, you must hit SHIFT and ENTER together. This adds a new line and does not execute the code. Remember to press enter to run the code after you have finished typing!

## Exercise

Try writing a knock-knock joke with alerts.

# Chapter 2: Variables AKA Boxes to Save Stuff for Later

**Variables** are used in programming to store and organize things. In Javascript, you can put just about anything in a *variable*; things like strings (text), numbers and more.

If it is not open, open the *console* and let's change up our first program a bit.

In the *console* type:

```
var welcome = "Welcome to my game!";
alert(welcome);
```

If typed correctly, you should see a small window appear that says "Welcome to my game!"

**var** is what is considered a **keyword**. *Keywords* are special words that programming languages use to determine what to do with the code next to them. In this case *var* tells the browser that *welcome* is the name of a new variable. To say this another way, you create variables by typing *var* followed by a name of your choosing.

There are a lot of *variable* rules, but for the purposes of this book, just know that variables should not be named after keywords and variable names cannot contain spaces.

You should typically keep variable names to words that describe the information they hold. In this case, the variable was named *welcome* since it held the message "Welcome to my game!".

You may notice that between the variable name 'welcome' and the text "Welcome to my game!" is an **equal sign**. In Javascript, the *equal sign* tells the browser to put the welcome message in the welcome variable. This in computerese is called **assignment**.

It is often useful to translate code into plain English to understand what is going on.

```
var welcome = "Welcome to my game!";
```

In english it would be: create a variable named *welcome* and put "Welcome to my game!" inside of it.

alert(welcome);

In english this would be: show what is inside the welcome variable.

It is also helpful to think of a variable as a box. When writing code, variables are great places to put things like *strings*. A big reason variables are used is to hold information that will change.

In the console type:

```
alert(welcome);
```

You should see "Welcome to my game!" appear. If you don't see it, it was probably reset by a page refresh. If this is the case, retype this in the console:

```
var welcome = "Welcome to my game!";
alert(welcome);
```

Now type:

```
welcome = "Welcome back!";
alert(welcome);
```

You should now see  "Welcome back!" appear in the alert box. By typing welcome without the keyword var, you are reusing the *welcome* variable you created before. This time you are filling it with a different message. In computerese this is called **reassignment**.

Now that you know about variables, the fun begins. With a little more work, we can build a game.

# Chapter 3: Game Time

You have already learned a lot; so much in fact, that we can start building a game. The *console* is a great place to type simple statements and commands, but it is no place for a full program. To help you get started, download the game kit from here:

**https://github.com/orangemantis/gamekit/archive/master.zip**

Once the game kit has been downloaded save it someplace you will easily be able to find it. The desktop or your documents folder would be a good place to put it. The game kit contains a bunch of useful resources and even sample code to help you if you get stuck. Many examples will be presented in this book. The code for these example can be found in the **gamekit/mygame/snippets** folder. The files are named after the examples.

As a new coder it is common to really mess up a file when trying something new. If you ever need a fresh start with a game kit file, simply grab a fresh copy from the game kit *archive* folder and save it to your game directory (the *mygame* folder). The archive is just a copy of all of the initial game kit files. **Make sure to never modify the archive files!**

Open the *gamekit* folder and then open the *mygame* folder that is inside of it.

Inside of the *mygame* folder, open the file named *main.js* using your text editor.

The *main.js* file, as the name implies, is the main program for your game. The *.js* tells the computer that the main file contains Javascript code. You do not have to worry about the other files in this folder; they are included to make your life easier. Programmers often depend on utilizing code that someone else has written. Think of these pre-written files as a library. In fact, that is exactly what a collection of prewritten programming files is called, a **library**.

Inside the main.js file you should see something that looks like this:

```
/* Add your code below */
```

This is called a comment. Comments begin with a slash and an asterisk and end with an asterisk and and a slash. Comments are notes in the code for people to read and are ignored by the computer. **Do not modify any of the code above this comment or any of the code below the comment that tells you such.** These comments are the boundaries for you to write your code.

---

**Note:** If you only have one line of comments you can use two slashes at the beginning of the line to create a comment.

```
//This is a single line comment.
```

Comments are important. Use them to describe what your code does. Comments serve another purpose too. You can use them to hide code from the computer.

Below the comment above in the main.js file, type:

```
/* alert("Hello World"); */
```

Save the file and then grab the *index.html* file from the *mygame* folder and drop it onto the browser window.

If you did things correctly, you should not see a "Hello World" alert box appear. The comment told the browser to ignore the code between asterisks.

The *index.html* is a web page. Javascript code needs a webpage to live inside. Before, when you were simply typing in the console, your Javascript was using the web page that was already in the browser.

If you were to open the index.html page with your text editor, you would see a few lines of HTML, one of them being something that looks like this:

```
<script src="main.js"></script>
```

This is a **script tag**. Tags are easy to spot as they all begin with **<** and end with **>**. HTML uses tags to tell the browser what to do. In this case the index page is telling the browser to get all the code in the main.js file and load it.

We aren't going to talk a lot about HTML since most of the HTML needed for this project is already included in the game kit. HTML is only discussed in this book to make things seem less magical.

Now that you know that dropping the HTML on the page will load it, you should know that once it is loaded, refreshing the page will show your new code changes. You can also bookmark the page so that you don't have to drag and drop it every time you want to view your code changes.

**Note:** You should know that if you bookmarked the index.html page, moving the files will break that bookmark. A bookmark is just an address that tells the browser where to find the file it wants to load.

Sometimes browsers will not see new code changes when you refresh the page. If this happens, you may need to empty your browser cache. The cache is a place where the browser saves files so that it doesn't have to constantly download ones that it doesn't expect to change. If you are using Chrome, you can type **chrome://history** in the address bar to open the the history settings.

On the left side of the browser click **history** and then click the button that says "Clear browsing data". A popup should appear with many options on it. Make sure that the box next to "Cached images and files" is checked and click the button that reads "Clear browsing data".

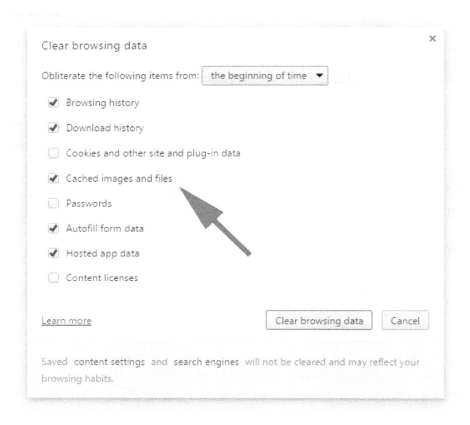

If you are not using Chrome, you may need to look online to find out how to do this for your particular browser.

Clearing the cache this way is good only if you have to make changes infrequently. Given that you will be making a lot of changes, it is better to disable the cache entirely. The Chrome inspector has a feature that allows you to keep the cache for a page disabled as long as the *inspector* is open.

To enable this feature, open the *inspector* if it is not already open.

Open the *inspector* settings by clicking the small gear pictured below.

In the settings panel check the box labeled "Disable Cache". Do not check "Disable Javascript"! Doing so will prevent any of the code you write from working. Disabling the cache means that the browser will show the newest changes from your files and not rely on the code it has saved.

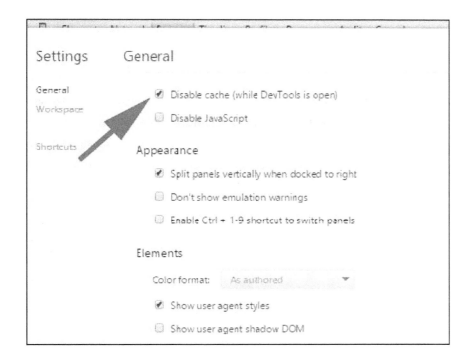

You can click the "X" in the upper right corner to save and close the settings. From now on, as long as the inspector is open, the cache will be disabled.

## Example 1

Open up the *main.js* file, remove the comment that contains the **alert** (do not remove any other code) and type:

```
/* Important game variable */
var myName = "Zultan Swack";
var title = "The Legend of Princess Helga";
var playerName = "";

var screen1Text = "Please enter your name:";
/* Show the game title." */
alert(title);
playerName = prompt(screen1Text);
```

Run the code above by saving your work and then refreshing the browser.

You may have noticed that we introduced a new method called **prompt**. Think of prompt as a cousin to alert. While an alert box only shows a message, a prompt is an alert that has a textbox inside of it. This allows the player to input data. In this case, the data the player is putting in is her name.

A prompt does something else that an alert cannot. A prompt will **return** a useful **value**.
One of the things that make functions special is that they can spit out data after they have done their job. This is called *returning* since it is giving back data. A *value* is simply one of the many words used that means data. In its simplest forms, *values* are basically letters, words and/or numbers.

We will talk more about data and *return values* later, but right now remember that if you give a prompt a parameter, it will use that as the prompt message. If a player types their name in the prompt text box, it will be saved in *playerName* variable.

If you wanted to see the value of the variable *playerName*, add the following to the end of your code:

```
console.log(playerName);
```

The console's **log** method is an easy way to print objects in the console. You can use this to display just about any valid Javascript in the console. This is a powerful feature. You can use this anytime you want to take a peek at what is going on in your code.

Refresh the page again, except this time when the prompt asks for your name, click *ok* without typing anything. Look at the value of the *playerName* variable again by adding the bolded text:

```
/* Important game variable */
var myName = "Zultan Swack";
var title = "The Legend of Princess Helga";
var playerName = "";

var screen1Text = "Please enter your name:";
/* Show the game title." */
alert(title);
playerName = prompt(screen1Text);
console.log(playerName);
```

The console should have displayed *""* after you pressed enter. Since you did not enter anything, an empty string is returned from the prompt.

At this point, you could let the player continue the game without a name. If you did this, anytime you would want to use the player's name, it would be blank. As a newly minted programmer, you cannot let this happen! You want to at least warn her that she didn't type a name. Fortunately, this is easy to do using an *if statement*.

## Example 2

Add the following bold text so that all of your code looks like this:

```
/* Important game variable */
var myName = "Zultan Swack";
var title = "The Legend of Princess Helga";
var playerName = "";

var screen1Text = "Please enter your name:";
/* Show the game title." */
alert(title);
playerName = prompt(screen1Text);
if (!playerName) {
        alert("You must enter a name!");
        playerName = prompt(screen1Text);
}
```

Refresh the page and this time do not enter a name when asked.

In the above code we used an **if statement** to check if anything was added for a name. The *if statement* uses the keyword *if* followed by parentheses that contain the condition you are checking. After the parenthesis is a **curly bracket** followed by some lines of code and then an opposite *curly bracket*. Curly brackets are the way that related code is grouped together in Javascript.

Code between curly brackets is often called a **block** of code. The block of code attached to the *if statement* only runs if the statement is true.

*If statements* only understand **true** or **false** and Javascript pretty much divides everything into one or the other. Imagine that the player typed "HANK" in the box when it asked for a name. **A variable that contains text is considered true.**

Since nothing was typed, playerName is "" and it just so happens that an **empty string (blank text) is considered false**.

We placed an exclamation point before the *playerName* variable and this does something that can be a little confusing at first. It allows *if statements* to treat *false* values as *true*. The exclamation point is called the **not operator**.

```
if (!playerName)
```

In plain english this says:

If *playerName* is empty (false) then do what is inside of the curly brackets.

This works since it is a true statement that the name is blank. Since the player's name equals false, the alert box is shown telling the player to enter a name. Afterwards, the prompt appears and asks for a name again.

```
if (!playerName) {
      alert("You must enter a name!");
      playerName = prompt(screen1Text);
}
```

You could also write this block of code as:

```
if (playerName === "") {
      alert("You must enter a name!");
```

```
        playerName = prompt(screen1Text);
}
```

The **triple equals** is how you check to see if two things are equal in Javascript. Remember, one equals sign sets a variable and three equal signs is how you check to see if two things equal each other.

Let's make sure that you get it. Open the console and type:

```
var test1 = "";
var test2 = false;
var test3;
var test4 = null;
var test5 = " ";
```

Then test each of these variables by typing:

```
if (!test1) {
    alert("This is false");
}

if (!test2) {
    alert("This is false");
}

if (!test3) {
    alert("This is false");
}

if (!test4) {
    alert("This is false");
}

if (!test5) {
    alert("This is false");
}
```

*test1* is empty text and is actually considered false. This alerted false.

*test2* is obviously false. This alerted false.

*test3* is not set and is therefore **undefined** and equal to false. This alerted false.

*test4* is **null**. *Null* means empty and therefore it is false. This alerted false.

*test5* was a trick. This one did not alert false, because it is not. If you pay careful attention you will notice that *test5* is one space, and a space is like an invisible letter. You may not have noticed it at first but it is there and that makes it true.

You learned a lot in this chapter and could technically write a game with all that you have learned. In the next chapter we will write a full but simple game using if statements, variables alerts and prompts.

# Chapter 4 : The Adventure Continues

You could continue to write the game from top to bottom, but this would present some challenges that would be nearly impossible to overcome. In the last chapter, you learned how to make sure the player enters a name. This works great if they enter a name the second time, but if they don't, then you have the exact same problem all over again.

To overcome this, you can create a rule that says if the player doesn't enter a name on the first or second try then she can't play. The rule would look like this:

```
/* Important game variable */
var myName = "Zultan Swack";
var title = "The Legend of Princess Helga";
var playerName = "";

var screen1Text = "Please enter your name:";
/* Show the game title." */
alert(title);
playerName = prompt(screen1Text);
if (!playerName) {
        alert("You must enter a name");
        playerName = prompt(screen1Text);
}
if (!playerName) {
    alert("Sorry, you can't play because you didn't enter a name, game over.");
}
```

While you could technically do this, this is not a good idea because it doesn't let the player enjoy the game simply because she made a mistake. Ideally, you'd like to tell her that she made a mistake and allow her to fix it so that she can continue playing. The way we are coding now doesn't allow this to happen. To make this possible we need to write some **functions**.

You have seen built in *functions* like *alert* and *prompt*, but up until now we haven't talked about writing your own. A *function* is a grouping or block of code that you want to reuse again and again. Functions are useful when you want to do the same thing in many different places. Instead of copying and pasting the same code again and again, you can write it inside of a function and reuse it.

## Example 3

To see a function in action, type the following in a new text document:

```
function myTest(name){
    if (!name) {
        alert("No name added.");
```

```
        }
    else {
        alert("A name was added.");
    }
}
```

Copy this, paste it in the console and hit enter. Now type:

**myTest();**

You should see:

Now type this in the console:

**myTest("Foo");**

This time you should see:

Several new things were introduced in the last example. Let's looks at them one-by-one.

A *function* is created or defined using the **function** keyword. This is followed by the name of the function. Functions can be named just about anything that is not a keyword. The function's name is followed by a pair of parenthesis. You can think of a function as a machine. Often, machines require you to put something inside of them to work. A lock needs a key, a car needs a driver and even a blender needs food to work. The parenthesis are a way to provide a function with anything it may need to work. In the example above, it needs a string.

The word inside of the function's parenthesis is a special kind of variable called a **parameter**. You use these just like you would a variable. The *parameter* can only be used inside the function. That means, even if it has the same name as a regular variable, it is actually different.

When you write the function's name and pass it parameters (without the function keyword), this is known as **calling** the function. When you *call* the function, you tell the browser to do what is inside of its definition. In the example above you pass in some text to the *myTest* function when it is called. This function has one job to do; it shows a message to let you know if any text was put into the name parameter. You already learned about *if statements*; what is new here is the **else** statement.

The *else* statement does what it says it does. It does something else if the *if statement* it is related to is false. You can only use an else when an *if statement* is declared above it. Again, the curly brackets ({ }) are how things like *if*, *else* and *function* keep code separate. You can think of them as a code fence. Everything between a set of them belongs together.

Functions will make more sense as you use them. Since you need the practice, create and call a function that tells a knock-knock joke. This shouldn't be too hard to do. Maybe you can reuse some of the code from one of the earlier lessons?

Now that we have covered the power of functions you can start to build a much better game. If your text editor is not open, open it and then open the *main.js* from the *gamekit/mygame* folder. This will be the home of your game code. Make sure this is saved in the scripts folder of your project.

## Example 4

Add the following code to the file:

```
var gameTitle = "The Legend of Helga";
var intro = "The princess has been kidnapped. You must save her!";
var playerName = "";

alert(gameTitle);
```

```
function askName(){
    playerName = prompt("Player what is your name?");
    if (!playerName) {
        alert("You must enter a name to continue.");
        askName();
    }
}

askName();

alert(intro);
```

This little snippet of code does the following:

It creates the variables that hold the title of the game and the intro text.  It also creates a placeholder variable for the player's name.

First the game title is shown.

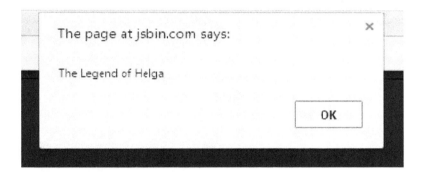

Afterwards, the *askName* function is created.  Right after this, the *askName* function is run (or called).  This is where some magic happens!  The *askName* function prompts:

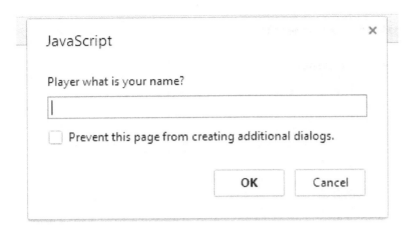

If no name was entered you will be alerted "You must enter name to continue.". The *askName* function is then called again to get the player's name. This will go on until the player actually types a name.

---

**Note: DO NOT** check the box that says "Prevent this page from creating additional dialogs." If you do this the game will not work. Checking the box prevents *alerts* and *prompts* from showing up. If you accidentally check the box, close the browser and reopen it. This will reset the browser's memory.

---

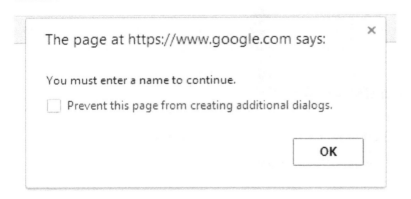

There is a technical word for this and it is called **recursion**. This simply means a function calls itself. *Recursion* is really cool and is used to make something in a program happen over, and over, and over, and over... again. Much like the last sentence, a function that uses recursion can go on forever. If you don't type a name, *askName* will just keep repeating.

Lastly, the game's introduction is shown.

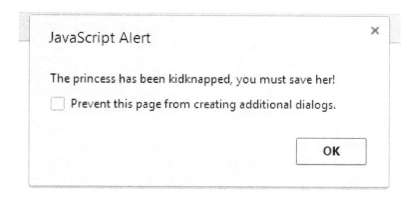

You learned a lot in this chapter and the game is really starting to take shape. Next up you will create even more functions to add more fun stuff to the game.

# Chapter 5: Building an Answer Screen

Text based games require players to type their answers on screen. The program figures out what to do based on what she has typed. To keep things simple you will only give the player 3 choices: A, B or C.

## Example 5

Add the following code in bold:

```
var gameTitle = "The Lengend of Helga";
var intro = "The princess has been kidknapped, you must save her!";
var playerName = "";

alert(gameTitle);

function askName(){
    playerName = prompt("Player what is your name?");
    if (!playerName) {
        alert("You must enter a name to continue.");
        askName();
    }
}

askName();

alert(intro);

/*Options screen*/
function playScreen1(){
    var screen1Text = "The princess is not going to save herself, " +
    "where will you start? \n" +
    "A) Venture into the Dark Forest \n" +
    "B) Visit the Dark Forest Temple \n" +
    "C) Quit";

    function checkAnswer(answer){
        alert(answer);
    }

    var playerAnswer = prompt(screen1Text);
    checkAnswer(playerAnswer);
}

playScreen1();
```

Wow, you just added a lot of code, don't be confused, let's break down what you just did.

The first thing you did was create a new function called *playScreen1*. This function handles asking the player what she wants to do.

Inside the *playScreen1* function (between the curly brackets) you created a variable *screen1Text*. Remember any variables created inside a function only exist inside that function. No other function can see that variable. If you typed `alert(screen1Text);` beneath the line that reads `playScreen1()`, you would see an error in the inspector because it cannot use variables from inside of a function that it is not also inside.

Try it and see what happens.

We have not done a lot with text yet but, things got a little complicated here. You could have typed the text as one very long line, but that could be hard for a developer to read. A way to break up text or strings into smaller lines is to use the **+ sign**. The *+ sign* is technically called the **plus operator**.

The *plus operator* is used to add numbers if you are doing math, but it can also combine text. If you want to stretch text over several lines of code to break it up, you must put a plus sign between the two pieces of text.

Both of the following work:

```
var someText1 = "Hello world I am here " +
"to stay for good!";

var someText2 = "Hello world I am here "
 + "to stay for good!";
```

If you pay close attention, you might notice **\n** inside of some of the text. This is a special way to tell the browser to create a **new line** on the screen.

To see it in action open the console and then copy and paste the following:

```
alert("Hello\n\n\n\n\n\n\n\n\n\nWorld");
```

You should see 10 lines between Hello and World.

You may have also noticed that inside of the *playScreen1* function you defined a *checkAnswer* function. This function is called after the player types an answer in the prompt.

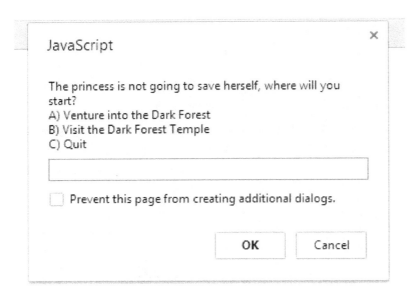

The *checkAnswer* function right now only shows what answer was typed. In the next section you will write some code that does something with the answer that the player types.

## Example 6

Add the following bold code so that your file looks like this:

```
var gameTitle = "The Lengend of Helga";
var intro = "The princess has been kidknapped, you must save her!";
var playerName = "";

alert(gameTitle);

function askName(){
    playerName = prompt("Player what is your name?");
    if (!playerName) {
        alert("You must enter a name to continue.");
        askName();
    }
}

askName();

alert(intro);

/*Options screen*/
function playScreen1(){
    var screen1Text = "The princess is not going to save herself, " +
```

```
"where will you start? \n" +
"A) Venture into the Dark Forest \n" +
"B) Visit the Dark Forest Temple \n" +
"C) Quit";

function checkAnswer(answer){
    if (answer === "A") {
        playScreen2();
    }

    if (answer === "B") {
        alert("You need a key to enter the temple");
        playScreen1();
    }
}

var playerAnswer = prompt(screen1Text);
checkAnswer(playerAnswer);
}

/*Option screen 2*/
function playScreen2(){
    alert("Screen 2 played.");
}

playScreen1();
```

The *checkAnswer* function you just added does what it says and it checks the answer typed by the player. In the first if block we compare the answer to "A" using **three equals signs (===).**

If you read the first *if block* in plain english it would say:
If the answer equals "A" (only uppercase) then call the *playScreen2* function.

In the next *if block* you are checking to see if the answer equals "B". If it does, you tell the player that she needs a key and then you show *screen one* again by calling *playScreen1*. We put the *checkAnswer* function inside of the *playScreen1* function so that we could send the player back to *screen one* if she gave a bad answer. This is *recursion* at work.

Congratulations, you just built your first full screen! We will use this technique in the next section to build a battle scene.

# Chapter 6: Creating a Battle

No adventure game can be complete without a battle. You may be wondering how a fight can take place when all you can do is type A, B and C. For this type of action you have to think less about video games and think more about traditional ones. Just for a moment forget about electronic games and think about board games. Think about an element of some board games that keeps play fun and unpredictable.

If you guessed the dice, you would be right. Dice are central to many games because the outcome of a roll cannot be predicted. The game you are creating is also going to use dice; not the real thing but a dice function. While we won't cover creating a dice function, you will use a prebuilt one.

Included in the sample code is something called **HelgaJS**. *HelgaJS* is a bunch of pre-written Javascript code that provides convenience and structure to building this type of game. This is included in the index.html webpage. *HelgaJS* has a method called **rollDice** that returns a random number between 1 and 12.

To see the *rollDice* method in action, load the index.html page and in the console type:

```
ge.rollDice();
```

Try the *rollDice* method several times to see the various numbers it produces. It should be really hard to produce the same number 3 times in a row.

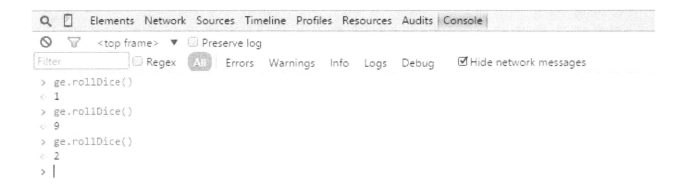

You might notice the *ge.* before the the *rollDice* method. That part is the **object** that *rollDice* belongs too. You can think of an object as a special variable that can hold many other variables and functions. When a function belongs to an object it is called a **method**. This may be confusing, but that is just the way it is. To add to the confusion, variables that belong to objects are called **properties**. Right now you don't need to remember all of that; all you need to know is that objects are full of information and functions. You get to the information in an object by typing a dot between the object and method (or property) name.

Technically, methods like *alert* and *prompt* belong to the **window** object. Typing:

window.alert("Hello");

is the same as typing:

alert("Hello");

Window is a special object that does not require you to type a dot to get to its methods. The browsers know that methods like alert and prompt belong to window. The *ge* object is actually attached to the window object. you could type:

```
window.ge.rollDice();
```

In your game you will use the *rollDice* method to determine things like the winners and losers of battles and if the hero can find items when searching for them.

## Example 7

Add the code in bold so that your file looks like this:

```
var gameTitle = "The Legend of Helga";
var intro = "The princess has been kidnapped, you must save her!";
var playerName = "";
var templeKey = false;
var lantern = false;
var hearts = 5;
var gems = 0;

alert(gameTitle);

function askName(){
    playerName = prompt("Player what is your name?");
    if (!playerName) {
        alert("You must enter a name to continue.");
        askName();
    }
}

askName();

alert(intro);
```

```
/*Options screen*/
function playScreen1(){
    var screen1Text = "The princess is not going to save herself, " +
    "where will you start? \n" +
    "A) Venture into the Dark Forest \n" +
    "B) Visit the Dark Forest Temple \n" +
    "C) Quit";

    function checkAnswer(answer){
        if (answer === "A") {
            playScreen2();
        }

        if (answer === "B") {
            alert("You need a key to enter the temple");
            playScreen1();
        }
    }

    var playerAnswer = prompt(screen1Text);
    checkAnswer(playerAnswer);
}

/*Option screen 2*/
function playScreen2(){
    var screen2Text = "The forest is dark and danger lurks ahead, " +
    "what will you do? \n" +
    "A) Look for a lantern \n" +
    "B) Look for a the Dark Forest Temple key \n" +
    "C) Quit";

    function checkAnswer(answer){
        var roll = ge.rollDice();
        if (answer === "A") {
            if (lantern) {
                alert("You can't find something you already have.");
                playScreen2();
            }
            else {
                if (roll > 6) {
                    lantern = true;
                    alert("You found a lantern");
                    playScreen2();
                }
                else {
                    alert("No luck finding a lantern, try again.");
                }
```

```
            }
        }

        if (answer === "B") {
            /*We will add this later*/
        }
    }

    var answer = prompt(screen2Text);
    checkAnswer(answer);
}

playScreen1();
```

There seems to be a trend with these examples; more and more code gets written every time! Let's break down what you just did.

You added four new variables: **templeKey**, **lantern**, **hearts** *and* **gems**. In this game, variables are the things that you use to remember if you have an item or not. When you create the *templeKey* and *lantern* variables they are set to false. This is how you create a placeholder for items. For any items that you plan to use, you need variables to hold them. You also set the variable hearts to five; this gives the hero 5 units of life. The gems variable is set to zero because the hero starts out with no money.

The *playScreen2* function has a variable inside of it called *screen2Text*. This variable has the text that is shown in the prompt. You did a similar thing in the *playScreen1* function.

You also created a *checkAnswer* function inside of *playScreen2*. Like in *playScreen1*, this inner function takes the answer the player gives and uses it to make a game choice.

Inside of the *checkAnswer* function, you created a variable called roll. This variable holds the random number returned from the *ge.rollDice* method. After this variable is declared things get a little tricky. You basically created a bunch of *if statements* inside of one another. To understand how this works, imagine a long hallway that has a series of doors that you must pass through. The hallway represents the path from the answer to an action. Each *if statement* is a door that can only be passed through when the condition is met.

In the first *if statement* you check to see if the player typed "A". If she did, the answer passes through to the next statement.

If the player has found a lantern, you show a message letting her know that she already has one and then you show the screen two choices again. Another fine example of recursion.

The *else statement* handles the scenario when the player doesn't have a lantern. This is where every player starts in a new game since the hero only has a sword and matches in the beginning.

Inside of the else you see:

```
if (roll > 6)
```

This uses the **greater than sign** (**>**) to compare the *roll* to the number 6. If the roll is greater than six, then the *lantern* variable is set to true. This gives the player a lantern. It then shows the player a message congratulating her. Afterwards it shows the *screen two* options again.

The *else statement* that follows shows the player an alert that basically says "tough luck" when the roll number is less than 6.

---

**Note:** If you are curious as to what the roll number is while you are testing, add the following code just below where you created the roll variable:

---

**alert(roll);**

You also added an empty *if statement* for the "B" answer. Don't worry, you will add that in the next section.

Lastly, you should see the code that shows the screen prompt and then the code that checks the answer. The check runs through all of the if/else statements described above.

Let's add the code to handle, if the player types "B". Hopefully most of this code will seem really familiar. Add the code in bold so that your file looks like this:

## Example 8

```
var gameTitle = "The Legend of Helga";
var intro = "The princess has been kidnapped, you must save her!";
var playerName = "";
var templeKey = false;
var lantern = false;
var hearts = 5;
var gems = 0;

alert(gameTitle);
```

```
function askName(){
    playerName = prompt("Player what is your name?");
    if (!playerName) {
        alert("You must enter a name to continue.");
        askName();
    }
}


askName();

alert(intro);

/*Options screen*/
function playScreen1(){
    var screen1Text = "The princess is not going to save herself, " +
    "where will you start? \n" +
    "A) Venture into the Dark Forest \n" +
    "B) Visit the Dark Forest Temple \n" +
    "C) Quit";


    function checkAnswer(answer){
        if (answer === "A") {
            playScreen2();
        }

        if (answer === "B") {
            alert("You need a key to enter the temple");
            playScreen1();
        }
    }

    var playerAnswer = prompt(screen1Text);
    checkAnswer(playerAnswer);
}

/*Option screen 2*/
function playScreen2(){
    var screen2Text = "The forest is dark and danger lurks ahead, " +
    "what will you do? \n" +
    "A) Look for a lantern \n" +
    "B) Look for a the Dark Forest Temple key \n" +
    "C) Quit";


    function checkAnswer(answer){
        var roll = ge.rollDice();
```

```javascript
if (answer === "A") {
    if (lantern) {
        alert("You can't find something you already have.");
        playScreen2();
    }
    else {
        if (roll > 6) {
            lantern = true;
            alert("You found a lantern");
            playScreen2();
        }
        else {
            alert("No luck finding a lantern, try again.");
            playScreen2();
        }
    }
}

if (answer === "B") {
    if (templeKey) {
        alert("You already have the key, head to the temple!");
        playScreen2();
    }
    else {
        if (roll === 3 || roll === 6 || roll === 9 || roll === 12) {
            templeKey = true;
            alert("You found the key!");
        }
        else {
            //fight here
            var roll2 = ge.rollDice();
            if (roll2 > 5) {
                gems += 5;
                alert ("You came across a Grublor and defeated it!" +
                        " You won 5 gems!");
                playScreen2();
            }
            else {
                hearts--;
                alert("You battled a Grublor and were hurt in the battle." +
                        " You lost a heart.");
            }
            if (hearts < 1) {
                alert("This was your final battle, game over.");
            }
            else {
                playScreen2();
            }
```

```
                }
            }
        }
    }

    var answer = prompt(screen2Text);
    checkAnswer(answer);
}

playScreen1();
```

The code keeps growing. Let's look at what you just did.

You first check to see if the player has found the temple key.

**if (templeKey)**

You check for this first, so that you don't have to write a check for this in every single block of code. Remember, it is always better to get things out of the way!

If the player has a key then you show her a message saying so. You then use recursion to show screen two again when you call:

**playScreen2();**

The else block is where the fun happens. You decide if the player finds a key, wins or loses a battle here.

In the first if block you check to see if the *roll* variable is equal to 3, 6, 9, or 12. If it is one of these, you give the player a key by setting the *templeKey* variable to true.

```
if (roll === 3 || roll === 6 || roll === 9 || roll === 12) {
    templeKey = true;
    alert("You found the key!");
}
```

This code uses a **double pipe (||)** in the if parenthesis. The || is the Javascript way of saying or. Technically this is called the **or operator**.

The *else statement* handles the roll if it is 1, 2, 4, 5, 7, 8, 10 or 11. This block is where the battle takes place. You roll the dice again and save the result in the *roll2* variable you declared. You then check to see if the *roll2* variable is greater than 5.

```
if (roll2 > 5)
```

If it is greater than five the player earns 5 gems by defeating an enemy named a Grublor.

```
gems += 5;
alert ("You came across a Grublor and defeated it!" +
" You won 5 gems!");
```

In the code above you use the **plus equals sign (+=)** to increase the value of *gems* . *Plus equals* is a way to add on to what you already have in a variable. Since the *gems* variable starts out at zero, the code above adds five to it. This is important; if you just use an equals sign you change the value of gems to 5 from whatever it was. This may not matter when a player has zero gems but what happens after they have won 50?

---

**Note:** You can also use *plus equals* on variables that contain text (strings). Try the following in the console to see what happens.

---

```
var test = "Hello World";
test += " is everybody's first program.";
alert(test);
```

The else that follows the block covered above handles if the *roll2* is less than or equal to five. In this case the player actually loses the battle and one heart as a penalty.

```
hearts--;
alert("You battled a Grublor and were hurt in the battle." +
" You lost a heart.");
```

We used a bit of Javascript magic to remove a heart. When you have a variable that contains a number you can add a **double minus** sign to the end of it to subtract one.

---

**Note:** If you add a double plus sign to the end of a variable that contains a number it will add one.

---

Try it out:

```
var test = 1;
test++;
alert(test);
```

The last *if/else* is very important. If the player still has hearts after a battle, you show screen two again. If the player's hearts are less than 1, then you show a game over message.

```
if (hearts < 1) {
    alert("This was your final battle, game over.");
}
else {
    playScreen2();
}
```

Believe it or not, you have learned everything you need to know to build a text based game. You could amaze your friends and family by building an incredibly fun and complicated game this way. There are, however, several reasons that you might want to build games in a different way.

For starters, this approach has a lot of repetitive code. Sometimes you have to rewrite similar code again and again. Some of this code you should be able to recycle. A different style of coding can make the amount of code you have to write much less.

This approach is also missing a lot of features. If you haven't figured it out by now, if the player types "a" instead of "A", the game just quits. No message, no warning, it just breaks. When things go wrong with a program it is always a good idea to tell the user something happened.

To make it easier on the player, you could force your game to accept lowercase and capital letters by writing something like this:

```
if (answer === "A" || answer === "a") {
    /*Do something here*/
}
```

This would allow the answer to equal "A" or "a".

You could also do something like this:

```
if (answer.toUpperCase() === "A") {
    /*Do something here*/
}
```

The code above actually makes the answer an uppercase letter and then compares it to "A".

While you could create a solution for each missing feature you find, there is a better way. You will use a library, specifically the **HelgaJS game engine** library to make your game coding task easier to manage. The HelgaJS library was written with only one purpose: to help new coders learn how to write Javascript by building a text-based game.

In the next chapter we will explore how to use the HelgaJS library to build your game. You will quickly learn it does a lot more than just roll the dice.

# Chapter 7: Introduction to the HelgaJS Game Engine

The HelgaJS game engine was created specifically to teach people how to write Javascript by building a text-based game. Text-based games are an excellent starter project since they don't involve graphics and can be built using minimal resources. There are no complicated thumb bending combos to memorized. There are only decisions to make and puzzles to solve. To use HelgaJS you simply need a text editor and a modern web browser.

## About the Legend of Helga

*The Legend of Helga* demo game is a light hearted homage to many of the great adventure games that involved exploring temples and rescuing a princess. The premise of the game and the play are simple. You are a young hero that is on a mission to rescue a princess from an evil king. You must explore a forest and ultimately a dungeness temple to find and save *Princess Helga*.

The hero begins the game with a pocket full of matches that burn out quickly as he searches for a lantern to guide him through a dark forest. If the hero runs out of matches before finding a lantern, the game is over. While on the quest the hero encounters enemies that threaten his survival. When the hero loses a battle his heart count goes down. When he wins, he is rewarded with gems. The hero can use the gems to buy things from the temple shop.

The temple shop has all the items the hero needs to improve his chances of defeating the evil King Malvox. The friendly shopkeeper not only sells wares, but also offers a few words of wisdom. To check the hero's equipment, the player can type "INVENTORY" or "STUFF" in the prompt. The hero must explores the temple in order to find treasure and the boss room. After the player finds the boss room and feels that she has equipped the hero well enough, the fight is on to save Princess Helga.

*The Legend of Helga* game should feel familiar and play should be easy and intuitive.

## Getting Started

1. First things first, make sure that your text editor and browser are open. We recommend Google Chrome for these activities but any browser will do.
2. Download the full HelgaJS sample code from:
   **https://github.com/orangemantis/HelgaJS/archive/master.zip**
   and save it to someplace convenient. Often the desktop is a good place.
3. Unzip the HelgaJS files.
4. From the HelgaJS folder, grab the index.html file and drag it onto your browser. This starts the demo game.

5. Play the demo until you either win or lose.

Helga JS comes with a demo game to help you understand some of the things that can be done using it. It serves as a good starting point for beginner and intermediate coders.

## How it Works

To play a game, game data must be created and then passed to the game engine through the *start* method. This is done by running the following command:

```
ge.start(gd);
```

The game engine appropriately named *ge* is the object that is responsible for controlling the game play. The game data is a Javascript object that at the very least requires the following properties:

**name:** The name of the hero
**hearts:** The amount of life the hero has
**gems:** The wallet for holding the hero's earned money
**enemies:** An array of enemy names
**_currentScreen:** The screen that the player is currently viewing
**_previousScreen:** The screen that came before the current one shown
**_gameoverWin:** The number of the screen that shows the message when a player wins
**_gameoverLose:** The number of the screen that shows the message when a player loses
**_quitScreen:** The message shown when a player quits
**screens:** The various screens shown as prompts (or alerts) to the player

## Example 9

Simple game data that only shows the title screen would look like this:

```
var gd = {
    name: "Roon",
    hearts: 5,
    gems: 0,
    enemies: [],
    _currentScreen: 0,
    _previousScreen: 0,
    _gameOverWin: 9999,
    _gameOverLose: 9999,
    _quitScreen: 9999,
    screens: [{
```

```
            id: 1,
            title: "The Legend of Helga",
            text: "Click OK to begin.",
            a: "",
            b: "",
            c: "",
            d: "",
            e: "",
            hideStats: true,
            action: function(ge, gd, answer){
                return {
                    goto: 9999
                };
            }

    }]
};
```

The *gd* variable holds an **object literal** that represents the game's data. An *object literal* is created by typing an opening and closing curly bracket and then assigning it to a variable. The creation of an empty *object literal*, or *object* for short, looks like:

```
var foo = {};
```

Object properties are specified within the curly brackets. They can pretty much be any valid string. The value of a property is declared after the name using a colon to separate the property name from the value. You can think of objects as super boxes that hold many other things. Properties are like variables that belong to the object they are created in. Objects help you organize code.

Properties can hold anything that a variable can, including functions and even other objects. HelgaJS uses objects to organize code into smaller chunks that make it easy to write and move around. Objects will be discussed more later on in the text.

The **screens** property of the game data object is where all of the magic happens. The screens property is an array of **screen object literals**. In Javascript, an array is a simple list. Items in an array are separated by a comma. Arrays are great for keeping track of things that have a numeric order. When counting the position of items in an array, you start with zero.

To create an array, type an opening square bracket followed by a closing one and assign it to a variable or object property.

```
var foo = [];
```

The following array has three different strings inside of it:

```
var foo = ["alpha", "beta", "gamma"];
```

The string *alpha* would be at array position 0, *beta* at 1, and *gamma* at 2. If you wanted to use any of the information in the array, you would get it using the numeric position.

To see this at work type the following in the console:

```
var foo = ["alpha", "beta", "gamma"];
alert(foo[1]);
```

The browser should say "beta". Since the variable *foo* holds the array, you use *foo* to access the values in the array. To get a value inside of an array, you type a set of brackets with the position of the item you want. There is a lot more to know about arrays, but this should be enough to get you started.

Try this again, this time show the word gamma.

Each **screen** is responsible for telling the game engine what to do. Below is a breakdown of what each property is for.

**id:** This property is not used by the game engine but it is used by you the game developer. It is just an easy way for you to know what screen you are working on. This should represent the numerical order of the screen in the *screens* property array. While array positions begin with zero, for the sake of making the game easier to follow, the *screen.id* should always be *array position* + 1. The game engine does the math when you reference the screen. It know that screen 1 is really at position zero in the *screens* array.

**title:** The text in this property is displayed on the first line of the screen shown to the player.

**text:** The text in this property is shown below the title.

**a:** The text for choice "A".

**b:** The text for choice "B".

**c:** The text for choice "C".

**d:** The text for choice "D".

**e:** The text for choice "E".

**hideStats:** This optional property if set to *true* will prevent the screen from displaying the hearts and gems.

**action:** The action property contains a function that tells the game engine what to do next. *Action* is passed three parameters the **game engine (ge)**, the **game data (gd)**, and **answer** (the answer player typed into the prompt).

The action method is where all custom logic is written to handle the flow of the game. Action returns an object that the game engine can use to automate certain common tasks. Below is a description of the properties that you can set in the return object that controls the game engine automation.

**goto:** This tells the game engine which screen to show next. This should be the *screen.id* number of the screen you want to show.

**hearts:** This tells the game engine to increase or decrease the hero's life. Positive numbers increase hearts and negatives take them away.

**gems:** Like hearts, you can use a number to increase or decrease the money the hero has earned.

The *action* must return an *object literal* with at least the *goto* property set to the number of the next screen to be show.

## Game Engine API (properties and methods)

The game engine has a few methods and properties that are used to make building the game easier. This is known as the **game engine API** (Application Programming Interface). *API* is a fancy word that means the thing you use to program the game engine. The API handle the more common programing task. Below is a list of the available methods and properties.

**addToken:** This method takes two strings parameters: *token* and *meth*. It adds the *token* to the *tokens* array and *meth* to the *tokenHandlers* array. This method can be used to add custom tokens to screens. See *tokens* for more information.

**adjustItem:** This method has two parameters: *name* and *val*. The *name* is a string that identifies a game data property. The *val* is the amount that should be added or subtracted from the game data property. This is used by the game engine to do things like subtract hearts when the hero is damaged or add gems when the hero finds money.

**attack:** This method has two parameters: *target* and *damage*. This method is used to reduce the hearts of game bosses or other enemies that have hearts.

**formatInventory:** This method is exclusively used by the game engine to create the text shown in the inventory screen.

**getBoss:** This method accepts a number that corresponds to the boss that you want to get returned from the game data *bosses* array. See bosses for more information.

**getCurrentBossName:** This fetches the current bosses name.

**getData:** This method returns the current game data that is loaded into the game engine.

**getEnemy:** This method returns an enemy from the enemy array based on the number passed to it.

**getItem:** This method takes a string name and returns the game data property that matches it. This is one of the most commonly used methods.

**getRandomNum:** This method accepts a number to use as an upper limit. When this is specified, a random number from zero to the limit will be returned.

**getScreen:** This method accepts a number and returns the screen from the game data *screens* array that corresponds to it. Unlike other methods that fetch items from arrays, the first item in this case starts with one and not zero.

**getScreenText:** This method takes the screen *title*, *text*, and *game options* and formats them for display on the screen.

**getStats:** This method grabs the current *hearts* and *gems* information and formats it for display on the screen.

**getTitle:** This method returns the *title* that is specified in the first screen. By convention the first screen should be the game title screen.

**getTokens:** This method returns the tokens from the token array. For more information see *tokens*.

**hasText:** This method has 2 parameters: *text* and optionally *textType*. The *text* passed to this method is checked to see if it is empty and contains more than empty space, often called white space (line breaks and spaces). The *textType* property when set to "ABC" will only allow letters. When it is set to "ABC123", it will allow both letters and numbers.

**parse:** This method takes two parameters: *txt* which can be any string and *tokens* which is an array of replaceable items. Parse replaces any tokens found in *txt* with the appropriate value. A good example of this is the player's name. Any text passed to *parse* that has the {{HERO}} token, is replaced by the value of the game data *name* property.

**process:** The *process* method is the main handler of screen actions. All of the game automation is done by this method.

**rollDice:** This method returns a random number between one and twelve.

**sellItem:** This method handles subtracting gems and placing items in the game data. It has two parameters: *item* (string) and *price* (number).

**setInventory:** This method adds an item to the inventory object. It has three parameters: *item*, *title* and *name*. The *item* is the string name for the inventory property. The *title* is the type of item that it is. The *name* is what the item is described as. In the case of the demo game, the hero has an sword item with "sword" as the title and "Silver Sword" as the name.

**setItem:** This method has two parameters *name* (string) and *val* (any type). It changes the value of the specified game data property.

**setTitle:** This method sets the title of the first screen. By convention the game title is set as the title of the first screen.

**showScreen:** This method is used by the game engine to show the screen specified. This method has two parameters: *gd*, the game data and *num*, the screen number to be shown.

**showScreenTmpl:** This method prints an empty sample screen object in the console. This is a convenience method for new coders that forget what screens should look like.

**start:** This method takes the game data passed to it, sets it in the engine and then shows the first screen starting the game.

**tokenHandlers:** This property is an array that should contain either a property name or function name that provides data for a corresponding *token*.

**tokens:** This property contains an array of tokens that are to be replaced in any screen text. This property along with *tokenHandler* is used by *parse* to format the screen text.

While it is great to read documents about how things work, it is often better to learn by doing. The sample game data (game.js) builds a full adventure game using the HelgaJS API and a variety of techniques.

To better understand how to use the HelgaJS engine, read through the sample game data documentation in the next chapter.

# Chapter 8: The Game Data Explained

## Screen 1

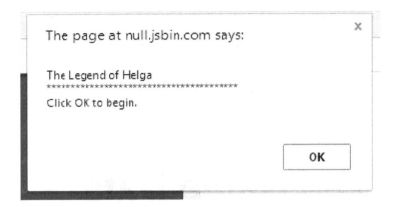

By convention, screen 1 is the the title screen. It is important to follow this convention as the *getTitle* Method returns the title from this screen as the game's title.

The action method of this screen adds matches to the inventory. The *matches* variable contains text that tells the player how many matches they start the game with. Notice that *getItem* is used to get the number of matches that have been set in the game data's *matches* property.

After the *matches* variable has been set, *setInventory* is called to add *matches* to the light category of the inventory.

The first parameter of *setInventory*, "light" tells the method to change the *light* item. At this point, the only inventory items shown on the inventory screen are light, key, sword and shield. The next parameter, "Light," sets the name of the display category. This could be set to anything you want to show on screen. Some might feel that it should be changed to "Matches". This is ok too. The final parameter *matches* sets the value of the matches variable as the description of the light item to tell the player how many matches they have.

Lastly, the action method **returns an action object** (RAO) that tells the game engine to go to screen 2. This is the heart of how the game works. You set the *goto* property of the object being returned to change screens.

```
//initialize inventory here
var matches = "Matches (" + ge.getItem("matches") + ")";
ge.setInventory('light', 'Light', matches);
return {goto: 2};
```

## Screen 2

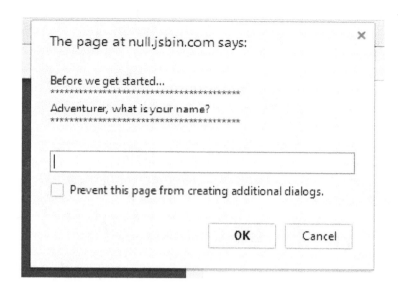

The page at null.jsbin.com says:

Before we get started...
\*\*\*\*\*\*\*\*\*\*\*\*\*\*\*\*\*\*\*\*\*\*\*\*\*\*\*\*\*\*\*\*\*\*\*\*\*\*\*\*\*\*
Adventurer, what is your name?
\*\*\*\*\*\*\*\*\*\*\*\*\*\*\*\*\*\*\*\*\*\*\*\*\*\*\*\*\*\*\*\*\*\*\*\*\*\*\*\*

☐ Prevent this page from creating additional dialogs.

**OK**      Cancel

The action method of screen 2 declares a blank return action object (RAO) upfront. This is done because this screen uses *if statements* to set the properties of this item, specifically the *goto* property.

The *if/ else* blocks in this method checks to see if a name was entered. If one was entered, the player goes to screen 4. If she doesn't enter a name she is sent to screen 3 where she will see a warning message that tells her that she needs to enter her name.

```
var act = {};
if (ge.hasText(answer)) {
    act.goto = 4;
    ge.setItem('name', answer);
}
else {
    act.goto = 3;
}

return act;
```

## Screen 3

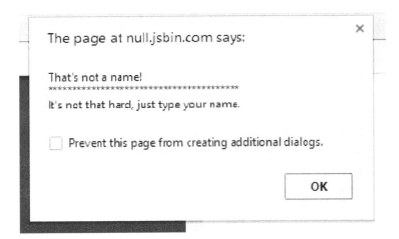

Not much too look at here, screen 3 shows a message telling the player that a name was not entered and then sends her back to screen 2 by setting the RAO *goto* to 2.

## Screen 4

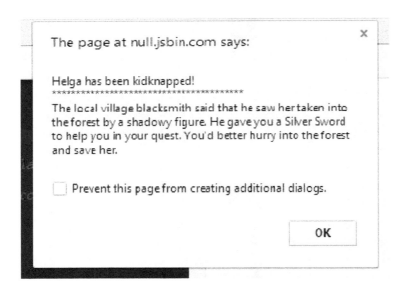

The *title* for screen 4 contains the *RESCUEE* replacement token. When the screen is shown the princess's name will be filled in.

title:"{{RESCUEE}} has been kidknapped!",

The action method for this screen simply sends the player to screen 5.

## Screen 5

This screen also replaces the *RESCUEE* token with the princess's name. It also sets the text for the various options.

The *action* for this screen is a typical example of how player decisions are handled. This screen uses a **switch** statement instead of *if/else*.

*Switch* statements are great replacements for places where you need multiple *if statements*.

*Switch* takes a parameter and it uses *case* statement to manage *if* conditions. In the code below we pass the *answer* to the *switch*. A *case* has a block of code that does something if the *switch* parameter matches the *case*.

In these cases (no pun intended), we handle if the player types A, B, C, D, STUFF, INVENTORY or anything else for that matter.

A case takes the form of *case* keyword, value to match and finally a colon.

**case "some value to match":**

This is then followed by lines of code that tell the game engine what it should do if the answer matches the values that follows the *case* keyword.

This screen's code sets *goto* to 7 if the answer is "A" and *goto* to 6 if the answer is "B". Notice that the *cases* for A and B both contain **break** as the last line before the next case. This tells the *switch* to ignore any of the *cases* below it. If no *break* is specified, each case below it will be applied if a match is found. This may seem odd at first but it can be useful as you will see with the "STUFF" case.

To better understand how this works, imagine that *switch* is a factory conveyor belt and the *cases* are workers that pull items and work on them if they match the value the *case* is responsible for.

The worker for *case* "A" only pulls items that match "A". Since this worker is instructed to *break*, this tells her to do her work (setting *goto* to 7) and then remove the item from the conveyor.

The worker for *case* "B" similarly grabs any matching item, does her job and then removes the item from the conveyor.

The "STUFF" *case* worker is different though. When she sees something that matches "STUFF", she does her job and leaves the item on the conveyor belt since there is no *break*. Since it hasn't been removed, it stays there and is handled by other *cases* until it reaches a *break* or the end.

In the code below, "STUFF" flows into the "INVENTORY" case. This technique is used to handle multiple answers that should have the same outcome. Without a break in the "STUFF" *case*, this allow the player to type "STUFF" or "INVENTORY" and have the same thing happen. When the player types either "STUFF" or "INVENTORY" *goto* is set to the number of the inventory screen. Since the inventory screen may be used all over the game, instead of having to look it up every time you need to use it, you set it as a game data property. This way you just have to remember the name of the property.

Lastly, the *default* statement happens when none of the other cases are met. If the player types anything other than "A", "B", "C", "STUFF" or "INVENTORY" the game uses the *getItem* method to get the number of the quit screen and sets *goto* to it. *Default* is the catch all for *switch* blocks.

```
var act = {};
switch(answer){
    case "A":
```

```
            act.goto = 7;
            break;
        case "B":
            act.goto = 6;
            break;
        case "STUFF":
        case "INVENTORY":
            act.goto = ge.getItem("_inventoryScreen");
            break;
        default:
            act.goto = ge.getItem("_quitScreen");

}

return act;
```

## Screen 6

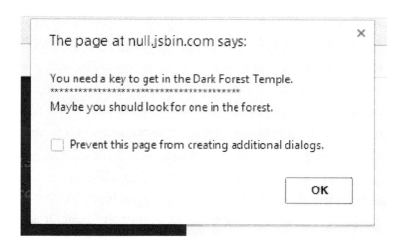

This screen is a simple message screen. The answer given on the previous screen isn't possible at this point in the game. This screen lets the player know that they need to do something to proceed. It just shows a message and sends the user back to the previous screen (5).

## Screen 7

```
The page at null.jsbin.com says:                           ×

The forest is dark.
*****************************************
you will need a lantern to find anything, what will you do?

A) Look for a lantern
B) Look for the temple key
C) Go to the Forest Temple
D) QUIT
*****************************************
Hearts: 5
Gems: 0

[                                                    ]

[ ] Prevent this page from creating additional dialogs.


              OK              Cancel
```

This screens declares the RAO as the variable *act*. It then declares a *lantern* variable and sets it to the the value of the the game data *lantern* property.

The lantern, like many other items in the game, is one that you either have or do not have. If you have a lantern, the value of the lantern property is true, otherwise (like at the start of the game) it is false.

A *roll* variable is declared and this uses the *rollDice* method to get a random number between 1 and 12.

The *matches* variable holds the current number of matches available. The *matches* variable, unlike the lantern, is a number that can increase or decrease. You do not have any more when the number of matches reaches zero. If that happens the game is over.

The *forestKey* variable gets the value of the *forestKey* game data property. This is a *true* or *false* (boolean) value like the lantern. You either have it or you don't.

The first *if* block tells the game engine to remove a match by setting the RAO *matches* property to -1. The game engine will add the number set here to the game data *matches* property. A negative number is used to effectively subtract one. If there is no lantern this action takes place after this screen is shown. The line that is commented out, is the manual way to remove a match immediately. You may need to do this manually if you have to add or remove items before the choices are processed.

The next *if* block checks to see if the player has either matches or a lantern. If the player doesn't have a light, *goto* is set to screen 11, a special game over screen. The *return* in this block stops the screen *action* from proceeding any further. The RAO gets sent back to the game engine and the game is over.

These actions happen before the player's answer is considered.

```
var act = {};
var lantern = ge.getItem('lantern');
var roll = ge.rollDice();
var matches = ge.getItem('matches');
var forestKey = ge.getItem('forestKey');

if (!lantern) {
    //ge.adjustItem('matches', -1);
    act.matches = -1;
}

//If there are no matches the game is over
if (!matches && !lantern) {
    act.goto = 11;
    return act;
}
```

The *switch* statement handles the player's answer. Answer "A" is to look for the lantern. If the player selects this, the first *if* statement of the "A" case checks to see if the player has a lantern. If she does, *goto* sends the player to screen 10.

The next *if* block only happens if the player does not have a lantern. It checks the *roll* variable and if the number rolled is greater than 6, the player is sent to screen 8 where she will be given a lantern.

The *else* block handles if the player rolled a 6 or less. This *else* block is contained inside of another *if/esle* block. This one says that if the player has any matches, she is sent to screen 9 to let her know that she has not yet found a lantern. Otherwise, she is sent to screen 11, the game over screen.

```
switch(answer){
```

```
case "A":
    if(lantern) {
        act.goto = 10;
        return act;
    }
    //Assume no lantern if here
    if (roll > 6) {
        act.goto = 8;
    }
    else {
        if(matches) {
            act.goto = 9;
        }
    }
```

In the first *if* statement of *case* "B" the code checks to see if the player has the *forestKey*. This is handled first to simplify the programming. If she has a key there is no need to do anything else. In this case, you simply tell the player that she already has one. If she has one, *goto* is set to 17. This screen just tells the player that she cannot find another key. The *return* here is used to prevent the function from executing any logic below. It is a big stop sign for the function.

**Note:** Remember, if you give a player an option, you have to let her know the result of her action even when she is not allowed to make it. Sometimes it is easier to give the player a choice and tell her that she cannot do it, than it is to remove the choice altogether.

The next *if* block checks to see if the dice roll is greater than 6. If it is, *goto* is set to 12. This screen tells the player that she found a key. When you design the game, you have to make your own rules that determine how players find things. In this case, rolling a number greater than six allows the player to find a key.

The else block that follows sets *goto* to 13. This screen tells the player that she has not found a key and she will have to try again.

```
case "B":
    if (forestKey) {
        act.goto = 17;
        return act;
    }
    if (roll > 6) {
        act.goto = 12;
    }
    else {
```

```
            act.goto = 13;//key not found
    }
    break;
```

*Case "C"* handles the action of the player trying to go to the temple. The *if* block uses the *setInventory* method to hide the forest key in the inventory screen since it has been used and is no longer available. The RAO *goto* property is set to 18 (the screen that shows the entrance of the temple). The else block handles if they don't have a key. It sets *goto* to 16, a screen that tells the player that she needs a key.

```
case "C":
    if (forestKey) {
        //hide key from inventory, it has been used
        ge.setInventory("key", "", "---");
        act.goto = 18;
    }
    else {
        act.goto = 16;
    }
    break;
```

## Screen 9

This screen is a message screen that tells the player that she did not find a lantern. The *if* block checks to see if there are matches. If there are matches, the player is sent back to the screen that sent her to this screen. The *else* block sends the player to a game end screen.

```
action: function (ge, gd, answer){
    var act = {};
```

```
    var matches = ge.getItem('matches');

    if (matches) {
        act.goto = 7;
    }
    else {
        act.goto = 11;
    }
    return act;
}
```

## Screen 10

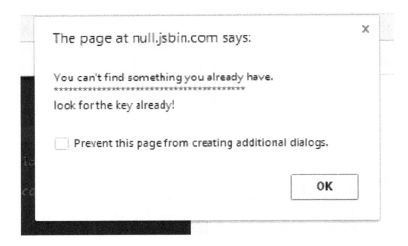

Screen 10 just tells the player that she cannot find another lantern and sends her back to the screen that sent her here.

## Screen 11

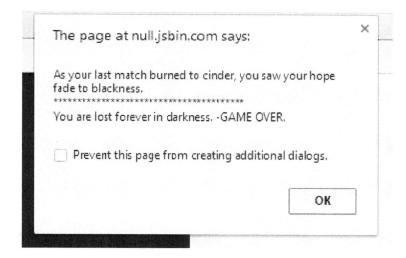

Screen 11 is a message screen that tells the player that she has used her last match. The *goto* is set to the game over screen.

## Screen 12

Screen 12 is a message screen that tells the player she found a key. The action sets the game data *forestKey* property to true and adds the key to the inventory.

```
action: function (ge, gd, answer){
    ge.setItem('forestKey', true);
    ge.setInventory("key", "", "Forest Temple Key");
    return {goto: 7};
}
```

# Screen 13

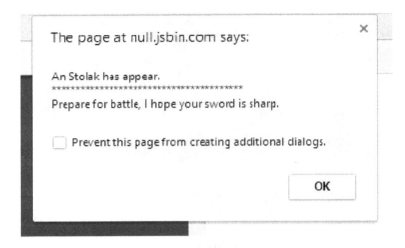

Screen 13 is a battle screen and handles the logic that determines if the player wins or loses.

```
action: function (ge, gd, answer){
    var act = {};
    var roll = ge.rollDice();
    if (roll > 7) {
            act.goto = 14;
    }
    else {
            act.goto = 15;
    }
    return act;
}
```

This screen also uses a dice roll to see if the player wins or loses.  If the player rolls a number greater than seven, she wins the fight and is sent to screen 14. This screen shows a victory message.

If she rolls a 7 or less she loses the battle and is sent to screen 15 which shows a defeat message.

## Screen 14

This screen shows the battle victory message for screen 13. For this win the player is awarded 5 gems by setting *act.gems* to five. The player is then sent back to screen 7.

```
action: function (ge, gd, answer){
    return {
       goto: 7,
    gems: 5
    };
}
```

## Screen 15

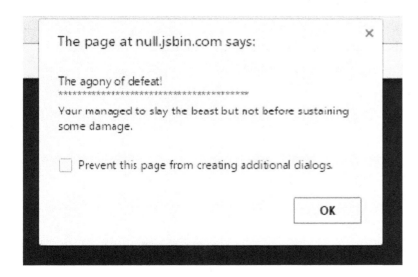

Screen 15 shows a defeat message from the battle waged in screen 13. It also removes 1 heart by setting *act.hearts* to -1. This tells the game engine to remove a heart. The player is sent back to screen 7.

```
action: function (ge, gd, answer){
    return {
    goto: 7,
    hearts: -1
    };
}
```

## Screen 16

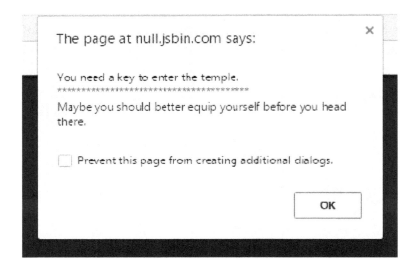

This screen tells the player that she needs a key to visit the temple and sends her back to screen 7.

## Screen 17

The page at null.jsbin.com says:

Tank you are not going to find another key.
\*\*\*\*\*\*\*\*\*\*\*\*\*\*\*\*\*\*\*\*\*\*\*\*\*\*\*\*\*\*\*\*\*\*\*\*\*\*
Is it time to head to the temple?

☐ Prevent this page from creating additional dialogs.

OK

This screen is a simple message screen that tells the player that she cannot find another key and sends her back to screen 7.

## Screen 18

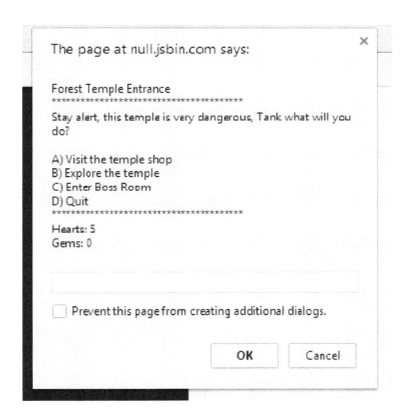

The page at null.jsbin.com says:

Forest Temple Entrance
\*\*\*\*\*\*\*\*\*\*\*\*\*\*\*\*\*\*\*\*\*\*\*\*\*\*\*\*\*\*\*\*\*\*\*\*\*\*\*\*\*\*
Stay alert, this temple is very dangerous, Tank what will you do?

A) Visit the temple shop
B) Explore the temple
C) Enter Boss Room
D) Quit
\*\*\*\*\*\*\*\*\*\*\*\*\*\*\*\*\*\*\*\*\*\*\*\*\*\*\*\*\*\*\*\*\*\*\*\*\*\*\*\*\*\*
Hearts: 5
Gems: 0

☐ Prevent this page from creating additional dialogs.

OK          Cancel

Screen 18 is the entrance of the temple and the next major action screen. Action screens follow a pattern that checks prerequisite conditions before any player decisions are even handled. There is no use checking the player's answer if the things that need to be done first have not been done.

The first *if* block sets up the temple boss. This is only run the first time this screen is shown. This is done by checking to see if a boss exists. The *getItem* method is used to see if the *_currentBoss* property is *false*. If it is false, this means that no boss has been set up and that it is ok to create one. The *boss* variable is used to hold the boss returned from the *getBoss* method. This method must be passed as a number that represents the boss you want returned.

---

**Note:** While arrays normally begin with zero, all game items start with one. This was done to make getting items from an array more intuitive.

---

A *bossKey* variable is created to see if the player has found a key to the boss room. The *lantern* variable holds the answer to whether or not the player has a lantern. The *act* variable is the same as it is in all the other screens. It is an empty object where the *goto* and other game driving properties used by the engine will be set. Lastly, the *roll* variable holds the number rolled by the virtual dice. These values are checked every time this screen is shown. This makes sure that the freshest information is available.

```
action: function (ge, gd, answer){
    //Set _currentBoss
    if (!ge.getItem('_currentBoss')) {
        var boss = ge.getBoss(1);
        ge.setItem('_currentBoss', boss);
    }
    //change screen text if boss key found
    var bossKey = ge.getItem('forestBossKey');
    var lantern = ge.getItem('lantern');
    var act = {};
    var roll = ge.rollDice();
```

*Case "A"* is simple, it sends the player to the temple shop, screen 19.

```
switch(answer){
        case "A":
            act.goto = 19;
            break;
```

*Case "B"* takes advantage of the true power of the dice roll and decides the player's fate when she explores the temple. The first if block checks to see if the player has a lantern, if she doesn't have one, a match is removed.

The next *if* block decides if the player will find a chest of gems. This block used a *double pipe* (| |), which in Javascript means *or,* to see if the player rolled a 1 or 12. If she rolled one of these numbers, she is sent to screen 26 to let her know that she found a chest of gems.

The next *if* block sends the player to screen 27 if she rolled a 9, 10 or 11. This screen tells her that she found a boss key.

The last *if* block sends the player to screen 28 for a battle if she rolled a 2, 3, 4, 5, 6, 7 or 8. Screen 28 is where a temple battle takes place.

```
case "B":
    if (!lantern){
        act.matches = -1;
    }
    // find chest
    if (roll === 1 || roll === 12) {
        act.goto = 26;
    }
    //find
    if (roll === 9 || roll === 10 || roll === 11) {
        act.goto = 27;
    }
    //fight here
    if (roll === 2 || roll === 3 || roll === 4 || roll === 5 || roll === 6 ||
        roll === 7 || roll === 8) {
        act.goto = 28;
    }
    break;
```

*Case "C"* handles when the player tries to fight the boss. The *if* block sends the player to screen 31 if she has the boss key. The *else* block sends the player to screen 32 to let her know that she needs a key to enter the boss room.

```
case "C":
    console.log('boss key ', bossKey);
    if (bossKey) {
        act.goto = 31;
    }
    else {
```

```
        act.goto = 32;
    }
    break;
```

## Screen 19

Screen 19 displays the temple shop. Every good adventure game needs a shop! This screen creates variables that hold the prices of everything sold in the shop. Variables named after the items were created to tell the engine if the player has the items or not. This is important since the rules of this game say that you can't sell the player something she already has.

By now you should be used to seeing the *act* variable. We won't mention this anymore.

```
var lanternPrice = 20;//20
var shieldPrice = 25;//35
var potionPrice = 15;//15

var act = {};
var gems = ge.getItem('gems');
var lantern = ge.getItem('lantern');
var shield = ge.getItem('leatherShield');
```

```
var potion = ge.getItem('heartPotion');
```

*Case "A"* handles the lantern buying logic. The first *if* block says that if the player already has a lantern, then send her to screen 20 and show a message that says she cannot buy another one. The accompanying *else* has an *if/else* inside of it that says if the player can afford the lantern send her to screen 21 to let her know that she now has a lantern. The *sellItem* method handles adding the item to the game data, but it doesn't automatically add it to the inventory screen. You can do this anytime using the *setInventory* method. The *sellItem* method returns true if the player has enough money and false if she do not. The accompanying else block sends the player to screen 22 if she doesn't have enough money to buy the item.

```
case "A":
    if (lantern) {
        act.goto = 20;
    }
    else {
        if (ge.sellItem('lantern', lanternPrice)) {
            act.goto = 21;
        }
        else {
            act.goto = 22;
        }
    }
    break;
```

*Case "B"* simply sends the player to screen 23. Option B is a trick of sorts. The player can never select this one. This is a taunt to the players that decided not to take the free lantern in the forest. Odds are the player will learn that after playing the game a few times, getting a lantern in the forest is the best option.

*Case "C" and case "D"* handle the logic for buying a shield and a potion respectively. This follows a similar pattern to *Case "A"*. All of these *cases* send the player to the screens that show the messages related to if she could or could not make a purchase.

## Screen 20

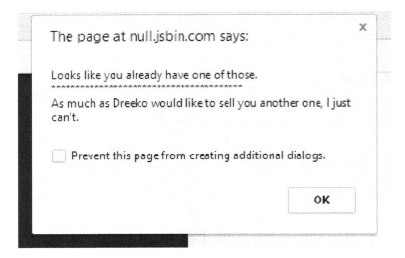

This screen is a generic message screen used to let the player know that she cannot buy the item because she already has one. This screen sends the player back to the temple shop. All of the shop related screens return the player back to the temple shop.

## Screen 21

This screen tells the player that she successfully bought a lantern.

## Screen 22

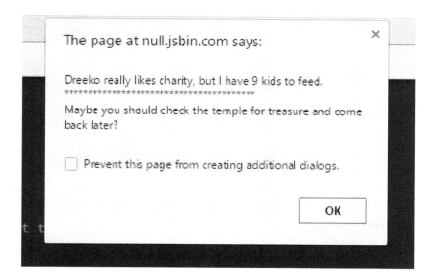

This screen shows a generic message when the player cannot afford to buy an item.

## Screen 23

This message screen gives the player a sarcastic message letting her know that even though she wants to buy matches, she should instead get a lantern.

## Screen 24

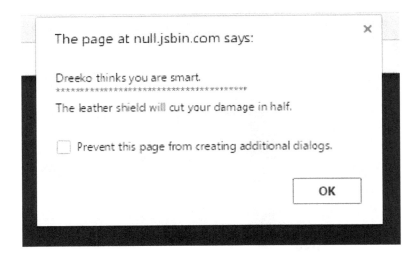

This screen lets the player know that she now owns a shield. It also lets the player know that she will receive less damage in battle because of it. The way that the game engine is written, if the player has a shield, it will automatically lower her damage. If you are interesting in taking a peek at that logic, look at the source code of the game engine *process* method.

## Screen 25

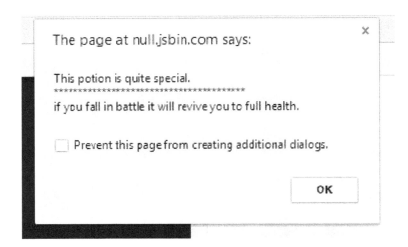

This screen is shown when the player has bought a potion. Like the shield, a potion works automatically. It is handled by the engine to make building a game easier. If the player has no hearts left, the potion automatically refills them. If this feature was not automatically handled, could you think of a way to do this?

## Screen 26

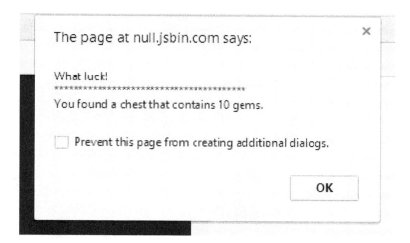

This screen is shown when a player on screen 18 decides to explore the temple and the roll says that she has found some gems. Gems are added by using the *adjustItems* method. This method can be used to increase or decrease items. Alternatively gems: 10 could have be added to the RAO.

```
ge.adjustItem('gems', 10);
return {goto: 18};
```

## Screen 27

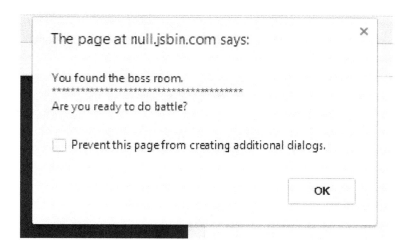

Screen 27 handles when the luck of the dice says that the player has found the boss room. The first line adds the boss key to the game data and the line that follows adds the boss key to the inventory screen.

```
ge.setItem('forestBossKey', true);
ge.setInventory("key", "", "Forest Boss Key");
return {goto: 18};
```

## Screen 28

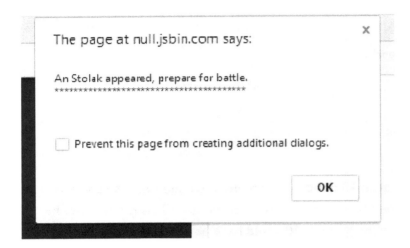

The code in this screen should look familiar, it handles a temple battle. This screen uses a dice roll to see if the player wins or loses. If the player rolls a 9 or greater she wins and is sent to screen 29. Otherwise she is sent to screen 30 to see a defeat message.

```
var act = {};
var roll = ge.rollDice();
if (roll > 8) {
    //win
    act.goto = 29;
}
else {
    act.goto = 30;
}
return act;
```

## Screen 29

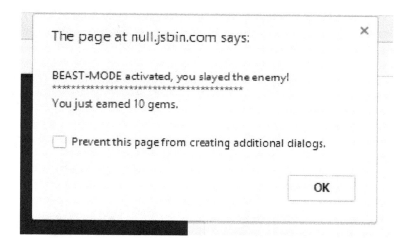

This screen lets the player know that she won the battle from screen 28. She is awarded 10 gems by setting the RAO *gems* property to 10.

```
return {
    goto: 18,
    gems: 10
};
```

## Screen 30

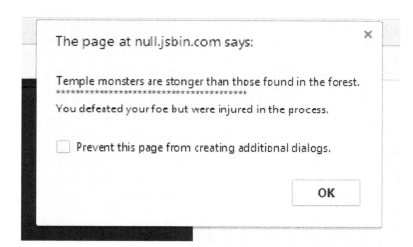

This screen handles when the dice says that the player has lost the battle. Damage to the hero is done by setting the hearts in the RAO to a negative number, in this case -2.

```
return {
    goto: 18,
    hearts: -2
};
```

## Screen 31

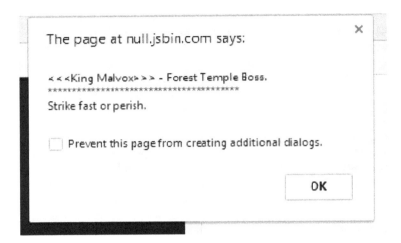

This screen is the boss room introduction. It lets the player know that a battle is about to begin. It simply sends the player to screen 33 to see the fight options.

## Screen 32

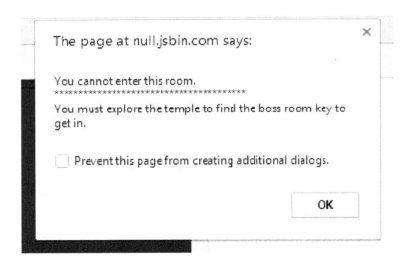

This screen tells the player that she needs a key to enter the boss room. This is shown when luck hasn't yet revealed one to the temple explorer.

## Screen 33

This screen handles the logic for all of the boss fight options. First, variables are set up to declare the RAO and a couple of dice rolls. Two dice rolls are used in the screen to add even more randomness to the fight outcome.

*Case "A"* handles if the player wants to use her sword. If she rolls a 7 or greater, she is sent to screen 34 where a success message will be shown and the boss will sustain damage from the attack. If the player rolls 6 or less, she is sent to screen 35 that shows a failure message and the hero sustains damage.

```
case "A":
    if (roll1 > 6) {
        act.goto = 34;
    }
    else {
        act.goto = 35;
    }
```

```
    break;
```

*Case "B"* handles when the player opts to try a special attack. Special attacks are rare and the code only allows a special attack to happen when both rolls are the same or both rolls added together equal 14. If either of these conditions is met the player is sent to screen 36 to inflict damage to the boss. It also lets the player know that she got lucky with a special attack. If neither condition is met, the player is sent to screen 37 where damage to the hero occurs. A message is shown to let the player know that the special attack failed miserably.

```
case "B":
    if (roll1 === roll2 || (roll1 + roll2 === 14)) {
        act.goto = 36;
    }
    else {
        act.goto = 37;
    }
```

*Case "C"* sends the player to screen 38 to let her know that she cannot win the game by dodging.

---

**Note:** You could add some risk to the hero by adding an *if/else* block that use a dice roll to determine if the dodge worked. This would add an element of danger to an otherwise safe option.

---

## Screen 34

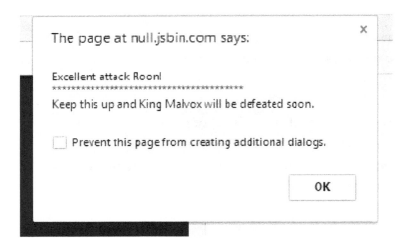

This screen creates a *boss* variable to hold the *boss object* retrieved from the game data. The *boss object* is a package of information about a specific boss. It tells the game engine the boss's name and how many hearts the boss has. The *act* variable holds a RAO with the *goto* set to screen 33. This assumes that the battle is still on and sends the player back to the fight option screen.

The boss object is required by the *attack* method. This method when passed the *boss object* and a negative number will remove the amount of hearts specified. *Attack* returns the number of hearts the boss has left. If the boss doesn't have any hearts left, the player is sent to screen 39 to see a victory message. By specifying the *goto* in the RAO upfront, the code assumes that the fight will continue. Doing this means that we only have to write code to handle when the the boss has no hearts and the fight is over. This technique can be used in many situations where there are only two outcomes. Just as easily you could have left *act* an empty object and created an *else* to set *goto* to 33 if the boss still had hearts.

```
var act = {goto: 33};
var boss = gd._currentBoss;
var bossHearts = ge.attack(boss, -1);

if (!bossHearts) {
    act.goto = 39;
}
return act;
```

## Screen 35

The page at null.jsbin.com says:

King Malvox is a skilled figher.
\*\*\*\*\*\*\*\*\*\*\*\*\*\*\*\*\*\*\*\*\*\*\*\*\*\*\*\*\*\*\*\*\*\*\*\*\*\*\*\*\*\*\*\*\*\*
You have been injured, I'm not sure how much of this you can take.

☐ Prevent this page from creating additional dialogs.

OK

This screen lets the player know that she lost the current fight with the boss. The *action* of this screen inflicts -2 hearts damage.

## Screen 36

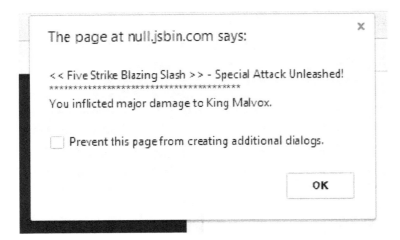

This screen handles the outcome of a successful special attack. The logic is almost identical to screen 34 except that instead of 1 heart damage, the boss loses 3 hearts in this type of attack.

## Screen 37

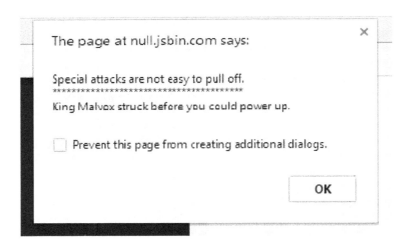

This screen shows the message that lets the player know that the special attack failed. The *action* tells the game engine to remove 2 hearts.

## Screen 38

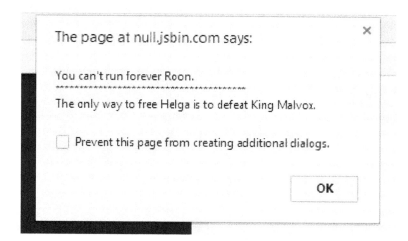

This screen tells the player that she will not win the game by dodging the boss.

## Screen 39

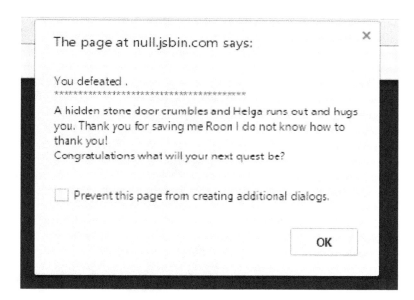

This screen handles the demise of the boss. The first line removes the current boss by setting _currentBoss to *null*. The next line does something really special; it increase the hero's total hearts by one. This is a useful feature for games that have more than one level. Typically, game difficulty increases as the game progresses. Bumping up the hero's hearts makes the hero strong enough to fight stronger bosses.

The _heartLimit property of the game data tells the engine the maximum number of hearts the hero can have. This code bumps up the limit by using the *adjustItem* method. The last line replenishes the hero's hearts.

The **ge.getItem('_heartLimit')** returns the value of the maximum number of hearts allowed for the hero. Another way to do this is to put the return value of *getItem* in a variable and then pass that variable to *setItem*. This code was written this way to show you that there are many ways to do the same thing.

```
ge.setItem('_currentBoss', null);
ge.adjustItem('_heartLimit', 1);
ge.setItem('hearts', ge.getItem('_heartLimit'));
```

## Screen 40

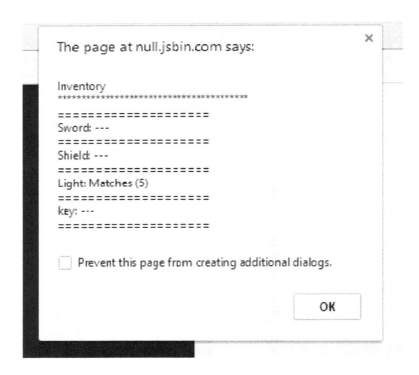

This screen is used to display the inventory. The *screenNum* variable represents the screen the player was on when she wanted to see the inventory. This is used to send the player back to that screen when the inventory screen is dismissed.

```
var screenNum = ge.getItem("_previousScreen");
return {goto: screenNum};
```

## Screen 41

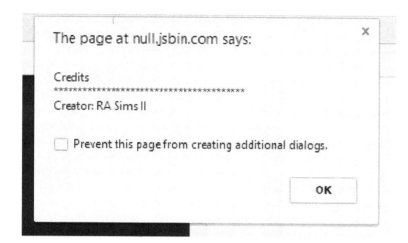

This screen displays the *credits* that are set in the game data credit property.

## Screen 42

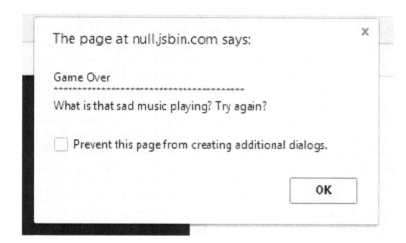

This screen shows the game over message for when the hero dies.

## Screen 43

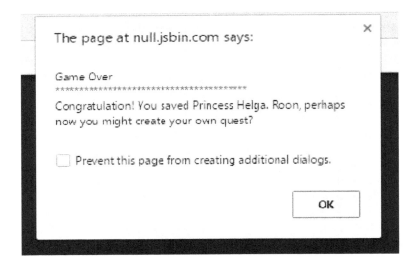

This screen show the game over message for when the hero defeats the boss and saves the princess.

## Screen 44

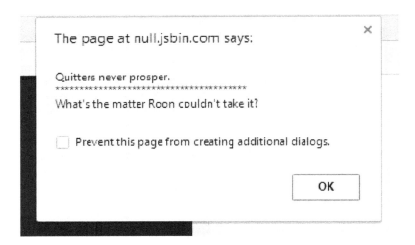

This screen shows the message when a player decides to quit the game.

You should now be equipped to create your own adventure game using the *HelgaJS Engine*. Even more, you should now know enough about programming to explore some of your own unique ideas.

You have only just begun on your programming voyage. Hopefully you will stick with it and produce something really cool.

Happy coding!

www.ingramcontent.com/pod-product-compliance
Lightning Source LLC
Chambersburg PA
CBHW060453060326
40689CB00020B/4509